Marbling on Paper
using oil paints

For Simon and Lucinda

Marbling on Paper
using oil paints

Anne Chambers

SEARCH PRESS

First published in Great Britain 1992
Search Press Limited,
Wellwood, North Farm Road,
Tunbridge Wells, Kent TN2 3DR

Reprinted 1996

Copyright © 1992 Anne Chambers
Photographs copyright © 1992 Search Press Studios

ISBN 0 85532 709 X

Composition by Genesis Typesetting,
Laser Quay, Rochester, Kent
Printed in Spain by Elkar S. Coop

Contents

Introduction
7

How to begin
9
Equipment · Materials
Marbling with oil paints

Traditional marbling techniques
21
Stone marble or splatter · Marble cut
Patterned · Combed · Stormont

Experimental marbling techniques
49

Using marbled papers
59

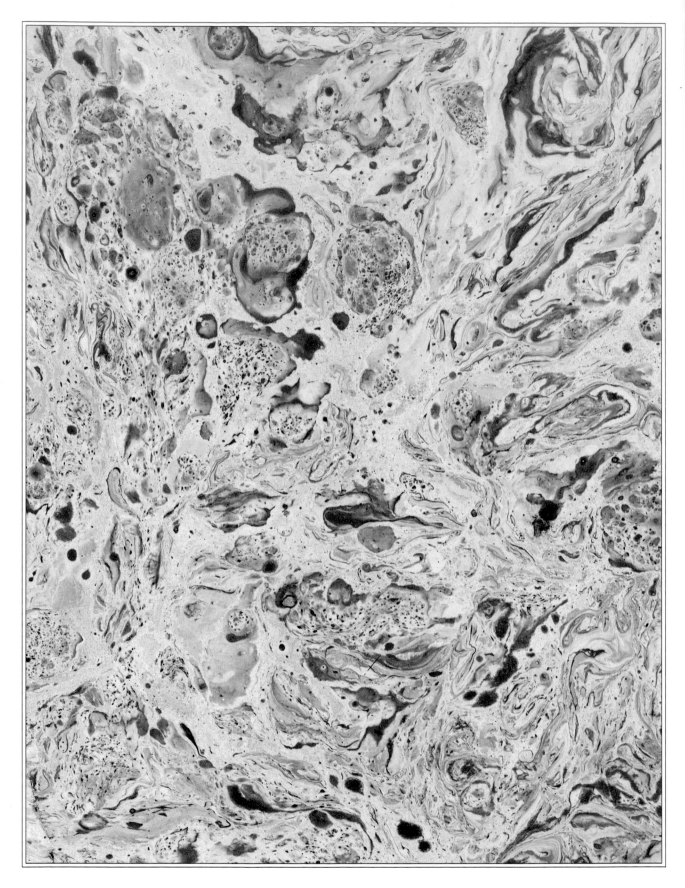

Introduction

Hand-decorated papers, made by various means, have been in use for many hundreds of years, and one of the most fascinating and extraordinary processes is known as marbling. To define this method simply, it consists of floating colours on a bath of water-based liquid, and then laying a sheet of paper on the surface, so that the colours are transferred to it. Each paper is different, because when the paper is laid down all the colours are taken up, leaving the surface of the bath clear.

Paper was marbled in this way in Japan in the early twelfth century (the art there is known as *suminagashi*), and a variation originated in Persia in the fourteenth century. Paper marbling then reached Turkey, where it was known as *ebru*, and was much practised and prized. From there the art spread throughout Europe, arriving in England in the sixteenth century.

Although marbling was no longer widely practised for a period before and during the Second World War, there has been a widespread revival of it, and it is used often for book-papers, decorative cards, and, in reproduction, for commercial packaging and wrapping-papers.

The early guilds of marblers kept their art a close secret, and marbled behind screens to maintain the mystery. Nowadays the secrets are more openly shared, and several books have been written on the traditional methods. The Japanese use calligraphy inks and pine resin dropped on a bath of clear water, the Turks a bath of gum tragacanth dissolved in water, and in Europe and America carragheen boiled up and strained is widely used as a base. In earlier times the colours were ground and mixed with beeswax, before adding ox-gall to break the viscosity of the bath, although nowadays water-based colours such as designers' gouache are simpler substitutes. Ox-gall is still used to disperse the colours, and the paper to be marbled is first sponged with a solution of alum to make it mordant. All this is quite complicated, and demands a degree of skill to ensure that the bath is of the right consistency and temperature, and that the amount of ox-gall added to each colour will enable it to spread correctly.

There is, however, an alternative method which is very simple indeed, but which can still give immediate and attractive results, and this is by using oil-based paints. Since oil and water do not mix, the oil paints, diluted with turpentine, will float on the surface of a bath of water, and these drops of paint can be manipulated with a stylus into interesting designs. To give more control to the manipulation of the colours, the water can be thickened with paste or gelatine. A little practice will produce a variety of effects, and contemporary marblers such as David Wade, who always uses this medium, have made very exciting papers.

There is a great deal of pleasure, and surprise, to be felt when one first uses this mysterious and magical process, and a great feeling of achievement as the papers are dried off and put to use.

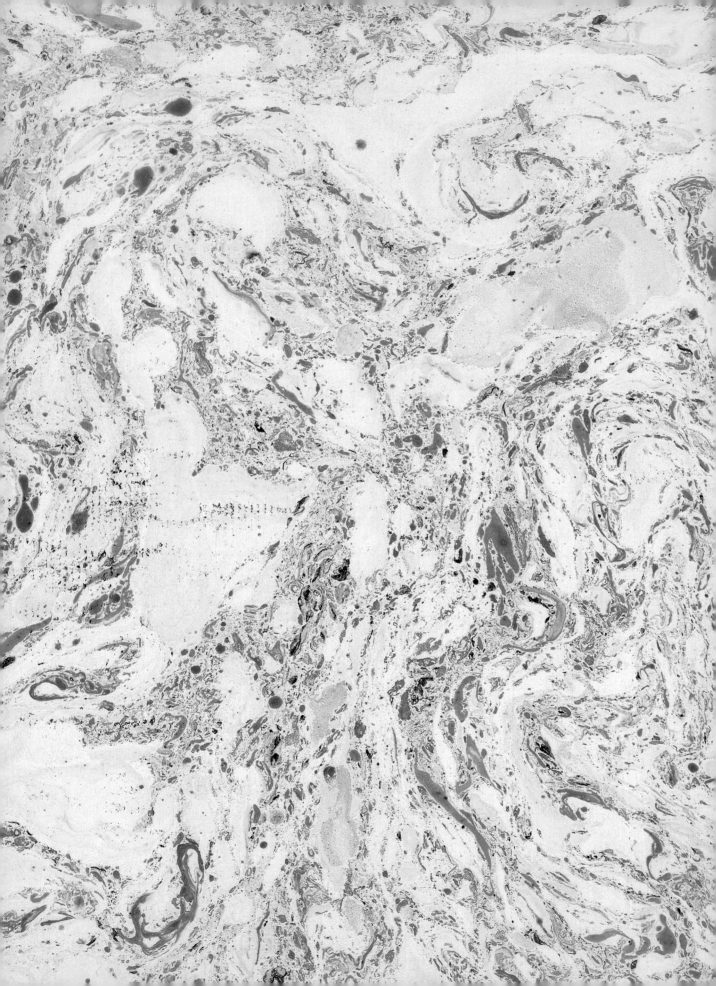

HOW TO BEGIN

How to begin

Marbling with oil paints need not be an expensive process, as many of the items needed can be improvised from pieces of household equipment.

Equipment

Work surface You will need a firm table or work surface on which to marble, covered with a plastic sheet or, failing that, clean newspaper. The floor should also be protected because drops of oil paint, not being water-soluble, are difficult to remove when dry, and you will be doing a certain amount of splattering whilst you work. For the same reason, do wear an overall.

Watertight tray This should be approximately 30 × 37.5cm (12 × 15in) and a minimum of 8cm (3in) deep. A plastic seed-tray or an old baking tin lined with foil will do well. More experienced marblers wanting to make larger sheets will find caterers' trays or photographic baths useful.

Pots for mixing paints Any small glass jars or old teacups will do, but I find it labour-saving to use yoghurt pots which can be thrown away after use. Disposable polystyrene mugs are not suitable, since the turpentine with which the paints are diluted also dissolves the mugs!

Brushes and eye-droppers Stiff brushes, 6mm (¼in) wide, are needed to mix the paint with the turpentine. These can be of the cheapest variety, with the over-long handles cut off, but should always be thoroughly washed after use with both turpentine and detergent, otherwise they will harden when dry and be useless. Glass eye-droppers can be bought cheaply from a chemist and are useful for dropping the diluted paints on to the surface of the bath. After cleaning they can be reused, although it is practical to keep one for each of the main colours, i.e. red, blue, yellow, green, and black.

Stylus, card, or comb A knitting needle, pencil, nail, or piece of stiff card can be used to manipulate the drops of colour, and a plastic comb with some teeth removed can also provide interesting effects.

Newspaper Apart from covering the work surface and surrounding floor area, newspaper is used to clean the bath between marbling by laying down a sheet cut to the size of the bath on the surface, and then lifting it off together with any remaining unabsorbed colour.

Rags It is important to keep your hands as paint-free as possible, so that the work stays clean. Rags moistened with turpentine are essential for this, and for quickly removing oil spots from unprotected surfaces.

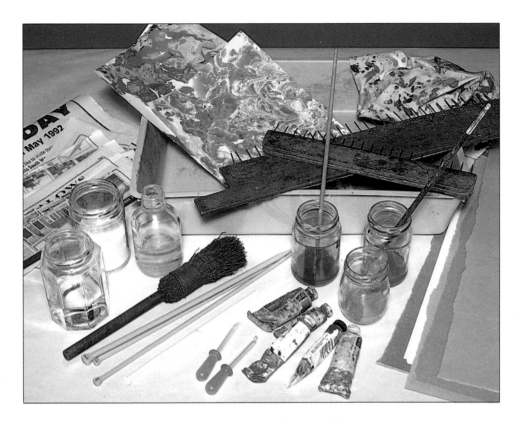

*A selection of equipment and materials required for oil marbling: oil colours;
detergent (washing-up liquid); wallpaper paste; turpentine; wide-toothed combs; eye-droppers;
newspaper; rags; watertight tray; paint jars; brushes; paper; knitting needles; straws.*

Materials

Water-thickener Although clear water can be used in the bath, if it is thickened
to the consistency of thin cream then the colours can be manipulated and
moved more easily. There are various thickeners. *Wallpaper paste:* Methyl
cellulose paste gives the best results, but an ordinary cellulose or cold-water
one will do. Ideally, when it is mixed to the required consistency it should be
left for a few hours, although this is not essential. Enough liquid should be
made to fill the bath almost to the top. *Cornflour (cornstarch):* Mix 50g (2oz)
with cold water in a saucepan. Then add 2 litres (4pt) of boiling water, and boil
for two or three minutes, stirring continuously. If the solution is too thick
when cold, then add enough warm water to make it the consistency of thin
cream. *Gelatine:* This can be obtained from any grocer's shop. Dissolve 25g
(1oz) in 50ml (2fl oz) of hot but not boiling water. When the gelatine is

completely dissolved, add sufficient cold water to make it up to 2 litres (4pt). The size should be liquid, and not set to jelly. *Powdered carragheen:* This can be obtained from art or craft shops, and should be made up according to the instructions on the packet. *PVA (polyvinyl acetate emulsion):* This can also be obtained from art shops, and should be diluted in water until a thin solution is obtained. This is a rather expensive way of marbling. *Gomme de guar:* Marie-Ange Doizey is a marbler who found a unique way of marbling, which she taught in France. She makes up a very stiff, almost solid, solution or size made from the powdered berry of a shrub found in India called *gomme de guar,* which is used commercially for stiffening fabric. She then paints strips of colour on the bath with wide thin brushes, instead of dropping on the colours. However, this method does require a certain amount of skill and experience (see page 51).

Paper I recommend good quality typing paper (bond, not flimsy), cartridge paper (not too stiff), writing paper, coloured sugar paper from art shops, and brown wrapping-paper. However, any paper which is reasonably strong and will not tear or shred when wet will be useful.

Turpentine to thin the colours This can be either pure spirits of turpentine, or turpentine substitute, but if the latter then do not buy a very cheap brand as it is not satisfactory.

Detergent (washing-up liquid) In addition to cleaning your brushes, after they have first been cleaned in turpentine, detergent can give some interesting effects if sprinkled on the surface of the bath (see page 51).

Oil colours Most manufacturers of artists' oil colours produce a range for students, in reasonably inexpensive tubes, which will work very well. It is, of course, possible to find every shade of oil paint ready for use in tubes. However, since paper marbling is a uniquely creative experience, each paper being absolutely individual to you, an extra sense of pleasure and achievement can be found in mixing your own colours, which can be very simply done.

I find that the true, rather hard colours such as pillar-box red (cadmium red) and royal blue (cobalt blue) do not lend themselves easily to mixing, and so I prefer to use a more subtle shade for these two primaries, although the true yellow (chrome yellow) is perfectly adaptable. The colours I like especially are rose madder (a particularly pretty dark pink red, rather than a scarlet), coeruleum blue (a lighter rather than a darker blue, certainly not a royal or indigo), and chrome yellow. If you cannot get exactly these colours, then try to find something as near as possible to them.

To start mixing, squeeze 6mm (¼in) of colour into the pot that you are going to use. Then, little by little, add your next colour until you have achieved the shade you had in mind. So, for example, to rose madder add yellow to create

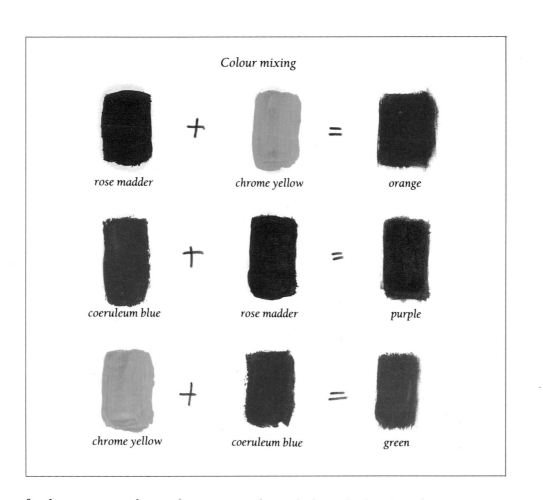

Colour mixing

rose madder + chrome yellow = orange

coeruleum blue + rose madder = purple

chrome yellow + coeruleum blue = green

firstly terracotta, then a deep orange, then a lighter shade. The same applies to blue: the addition of yellow in varying amounts will give you shades of green ranging from leaf-green to turquoise. Blue with rose madder will give shades of violet and purple. In turn, all of these colours can be varied enormously by the addition of white. Make sure that the colours are completely mixed, and not streaky. Once the colour is satisfactory, it must be diluted with turpentine to make it liquid enough for use (see page 14).

Of course, there are times, especially when doing experimental rather than traditional marbling, when you will want to use very bold, hard colours, so obviously you will need these in your collection as well; black is also useful for a strong contrasting colour. However, with perhaps a total of only eight well-chosen tubes you can create an extremely varied and contrasting amount of papers.

Marbling with oil paints

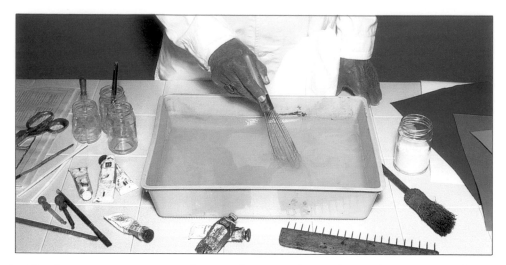

1. Firstly, prepare your work area by spreading plastic sheeting or clean newspaper on the work surface and the floor surrounding. Then, fill the bath with the prepared size (see pages 11–12) to a depth of at least 6cm (2½in). Check the size to ensure that it is of the correct consistency.

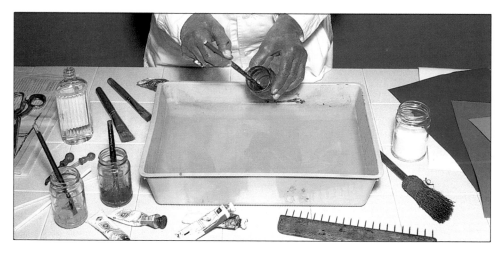

2. Mix up two or three colours by squeezing about 6mm (¼in) from the tube of paint, and diluting this with a few drops of spirits of turpentine or turpentine substitute. With a small stiff paintbrush, work the spirit well into the paint to soften and dissolve it. Do not add more than a few drops, or it will be difficult to dissolve the oil paint satisfactorily. When it is completely smooth, add more spirit, little by little, stirring continuously, until the colour is liquid enough to drop from the brush, or be taken up in an eye-dropper. Each colour should have its own brush, or eye-dropper, resting in the pot or jar. Line these jars alongside the bath, conveniently to hand.

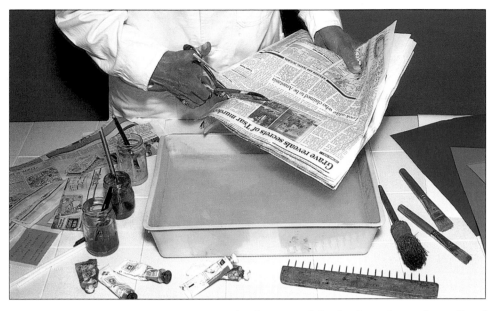

3. Cut or tear pieces of newspaper to fit the size of the bath, and another pile of strips about 7cm (2¾in) deep to fit the width of the bath. Put the pile of paper to be marbled a little way away from the bath, so that it will not get splattered inadvertently. Have some rags moistened with turpentine substitute nearby to clean your hands and mop up any stray drops of paint, and a plastic bucket or bin for used paper. Have to hand also the stylus, pencil, or nail you will use to distribute the colours on the surface of the bath.

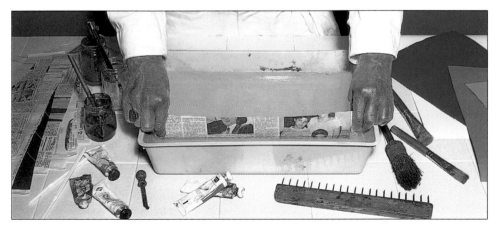

4. Now you are ready to begin. Skim the surface of the bath with a strip of paper to remove the surface tension which has built up on the size. If this is not done, then the colours will not spread satisfactorily.

5. Sprinkle drops of the first colour at random over the bath. If the colour fails to spread adequately to circles of about 2.5cm (1in) or so, then add more spirit. If it spreads too violently, then it has too much spirit, and more colour will have to be added very carefully and worked well in.

6. If, however, the drops of colour spread well all over the bath, then drop on your next colour, and if that works well, add your third.

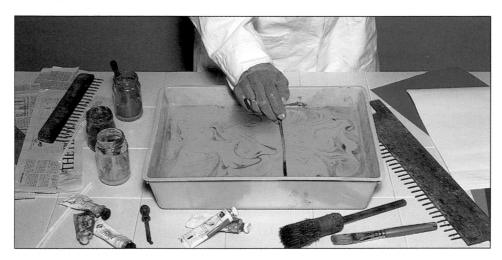

7. Then, with the stylus, gently manoeuvre the colours to achieve a swirled effect. The colours will not merge with each other when you draw the stylus gently through them, but will remain separate.

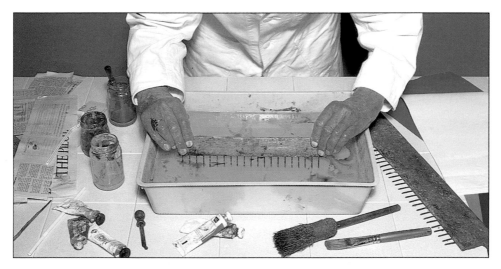

8. You can also manipulate the colours with a piece of stiff card or, when you are a little more experienced, try to comb them through with a widely spaced plastic comb, touching this lightly to the surface of the water and not dragging it through. If you do not like the pattern you have made on the surface, then you can remove it very easily by laying down a sheet of newspaper on the bath, which will absorb or remove all of the colours.

9. When you are satisfied with the pattern, wipe your hands clean of any paint, and pick up a clean sheet of paper from the pile. It must be laid down carefully on the surface to ensure that no air bubbles are entrapped, as any pockets of air would prevent the colour from adhering to the paper at these points. Pick up the sheet by the top left and bottom right corners, and, starting from the bottom right, lay the sheet down diagonally on the surface of the bath. As you lay the paper slowly and carefully down on the surface, you can observe a distinct shadow on the under-side of the paper as it picks up the size.

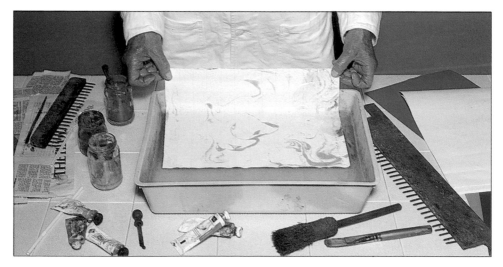

10. Once the paper is lying flat on the surface, pick up the bottom left and bottom right-hand corners (those nearest to you) and pull the paper gently over the rim of the bath, so that the slime is scraped off as the paper is pulled out of the water.

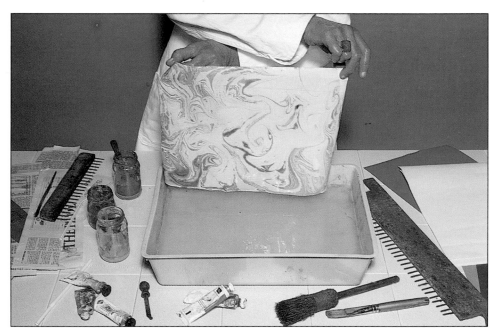

11. Lay the paper marbled side up on newspaper to dry flat, or peg it to a line. When it is absolutely dry it can be pressed under boards, but remember that oil paints take much longer to dry than water paints.

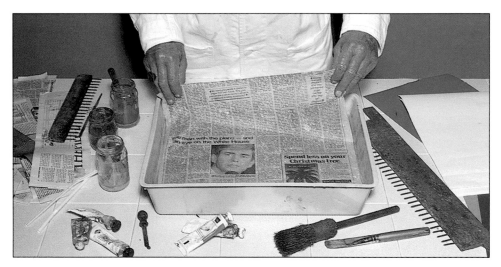

12. If any spots of paint are left on the surface of the bath, then clean it by putting down a piece of newspaper on the surface. The surface should be skimmed with a strip of newspaper before starting to marble again.

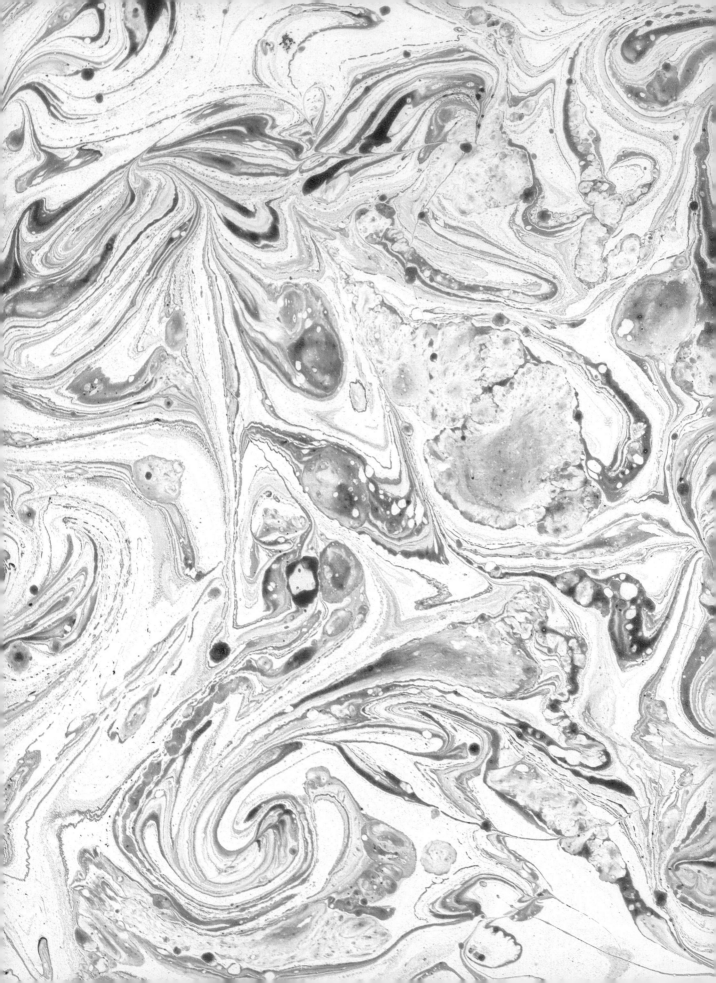

TRADITIONAL MARBLING TECHNIQUES

Blue, rose.

Traditional marbling techniques

There are various traditional marbled papers, known by names such as Antique spot, French shell, Italian shell, Stormont, and French curl or snail. In oil marbling, it is possible to emulate some of these patterns quite successfully with a little practice. In this section, five variations are described, and within these categories distinctive patterns may be made. It is advisable to make notes of colours used, and designs made, at the time of marbling, as it is not always easy to recall exactly what the process was when you want to repeat the design. Also, if you particularly like a sheet you have done, then repeat it several times, as you will probably need several pieces of it for book covering or suchlike.

Stone marble or splatter

This is the basic form, and from this other papers, such as patterned or combed, are made. Two or three colours are thrown at random on to the surface of the bath, using a brush, whisk, or eye-droppers. Variations can be made by adding more turpentine to the third colour, so that it will spread widely, causing the first two colours to close up and become dense, forming what are called vein colours. The colours thrown on can be manipulated with a stylus or piece of stiff card.

An example of a stone marble pattern as it appears on the surface of the bath.

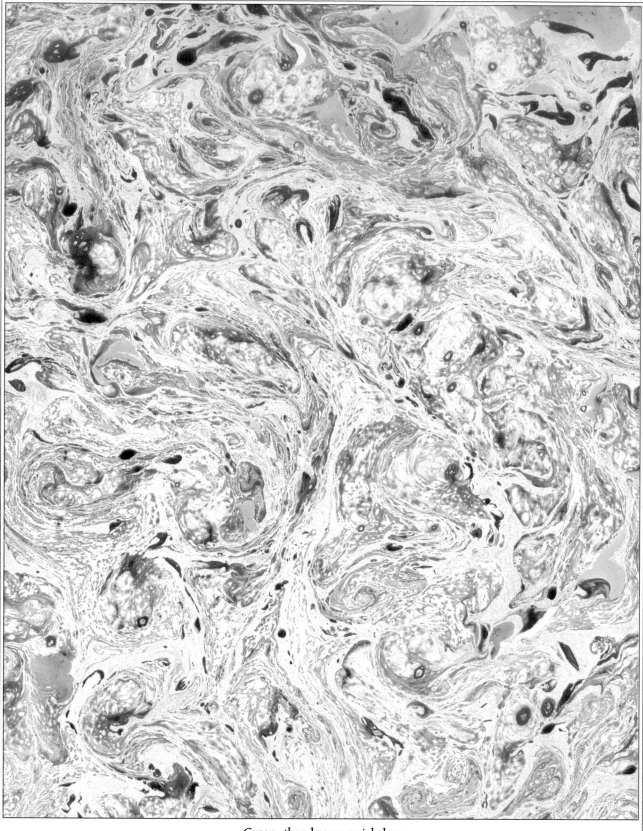

Green, then brown swirled on.

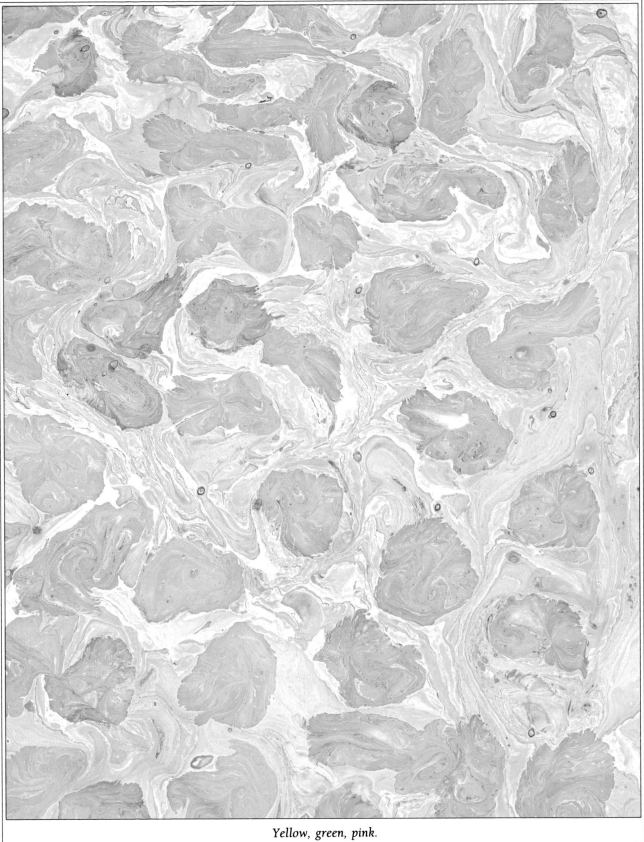

Yellow, green, pink.

[25]

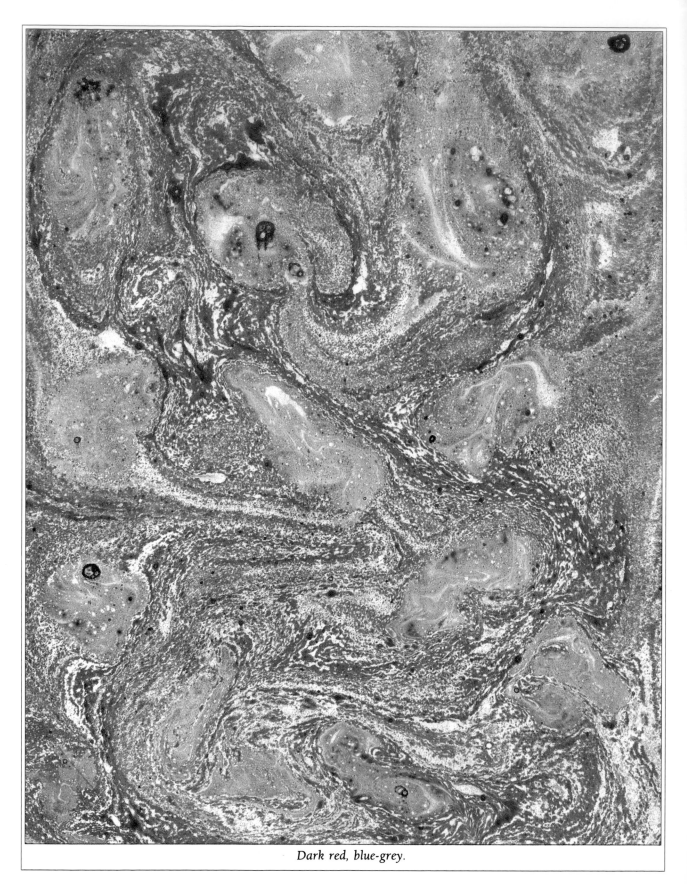

Dark red, blue-grey.

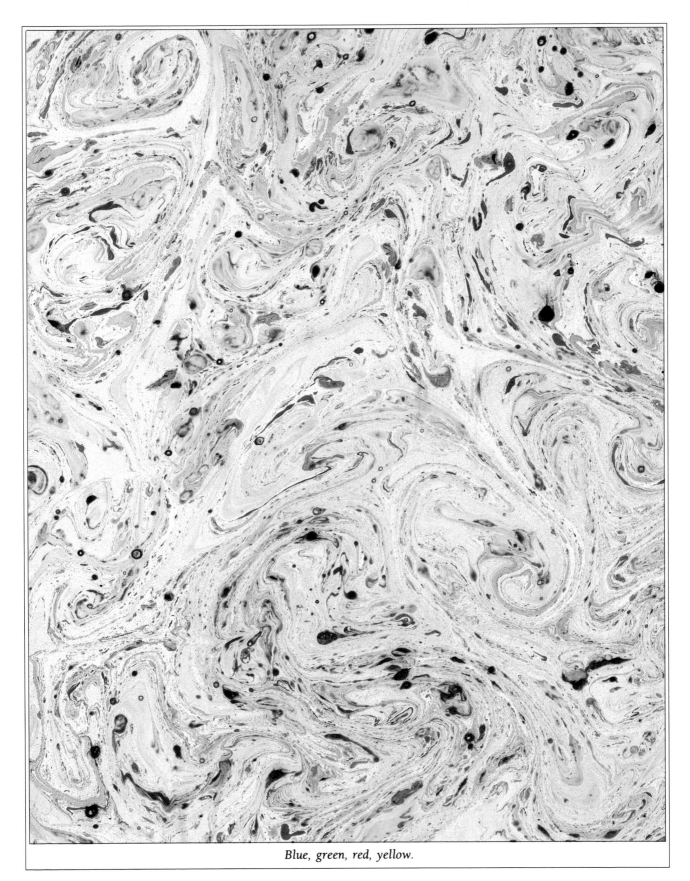

Blue, green, red, yellow.

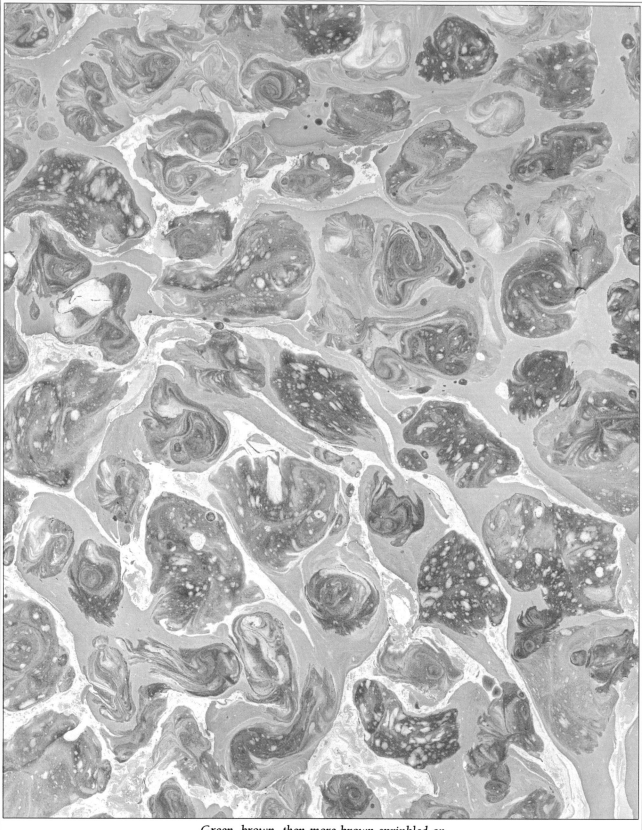

Green, brown, then more brown sprinkled on.

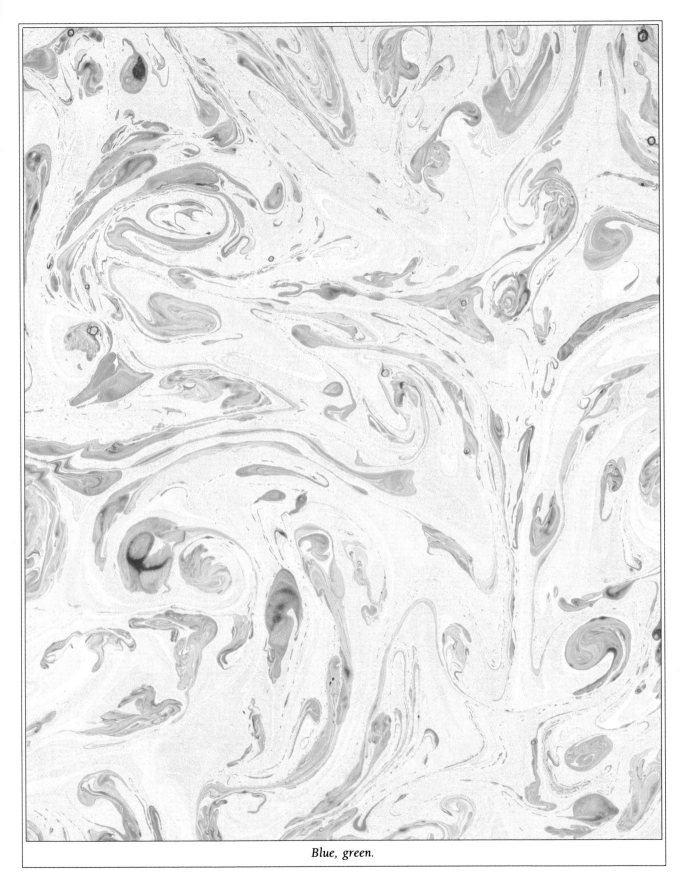

Blue, green.

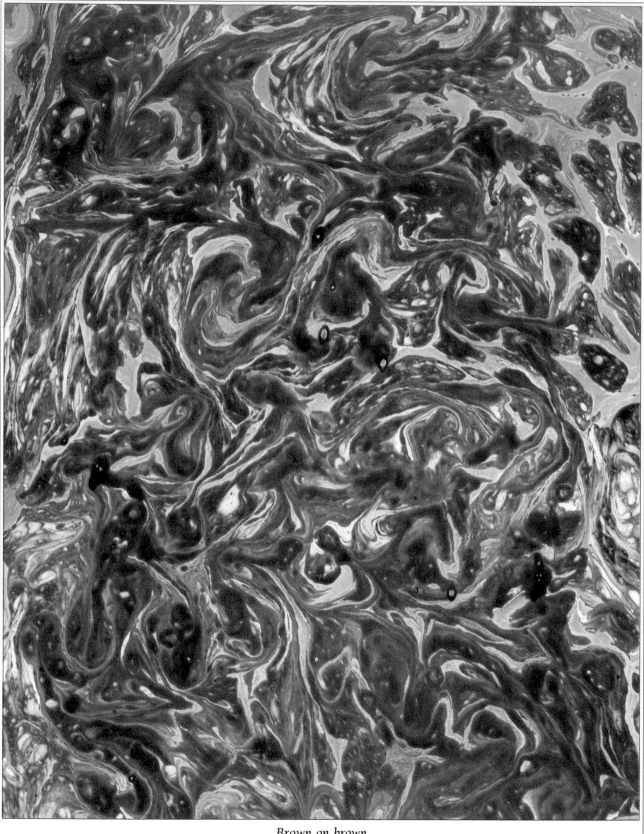

Brown on brown.

Marble cut

Here, one colour only is used, to which sufficient turpentine is added to make it spread quickly over the entire surface of the bath. The colour may then be thrown again on this surface, although this time it will be inhibited by the colour already on the surface of the bath, and so will form much smaller drops. With a stylus, the colour is then gently swirled about, to create a monotone marbled effect.

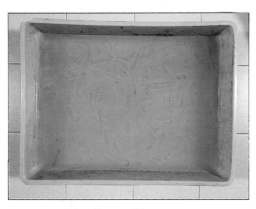

An example of a marble cut pattern as it appears on the surface of the bath.

Rose.

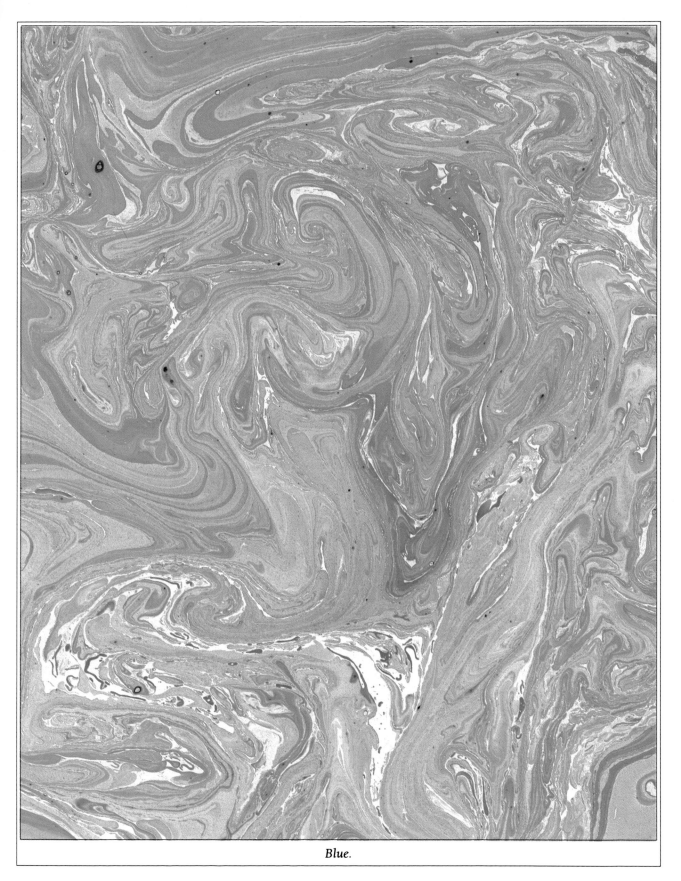

Blue.

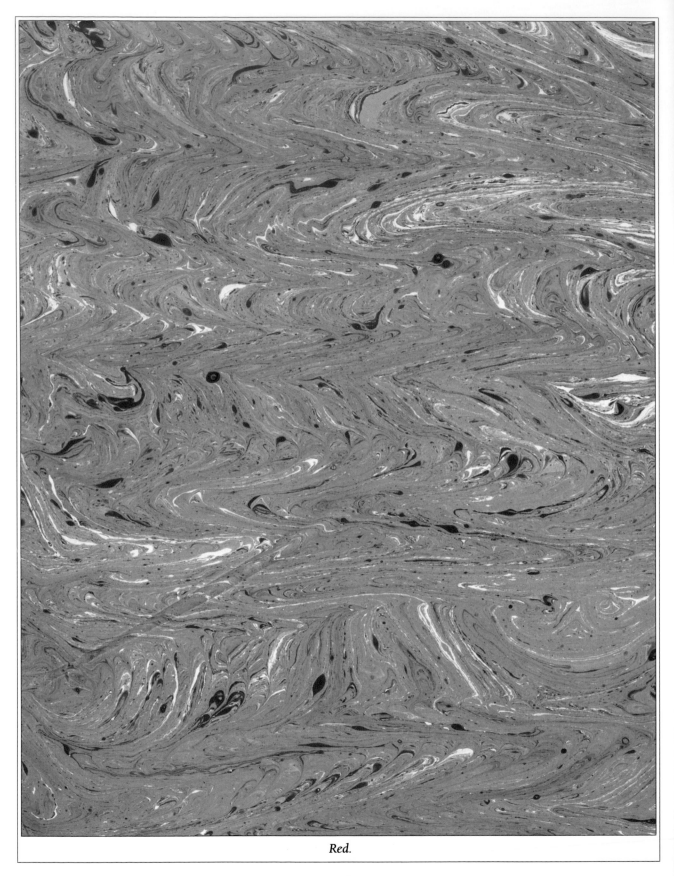

Red.

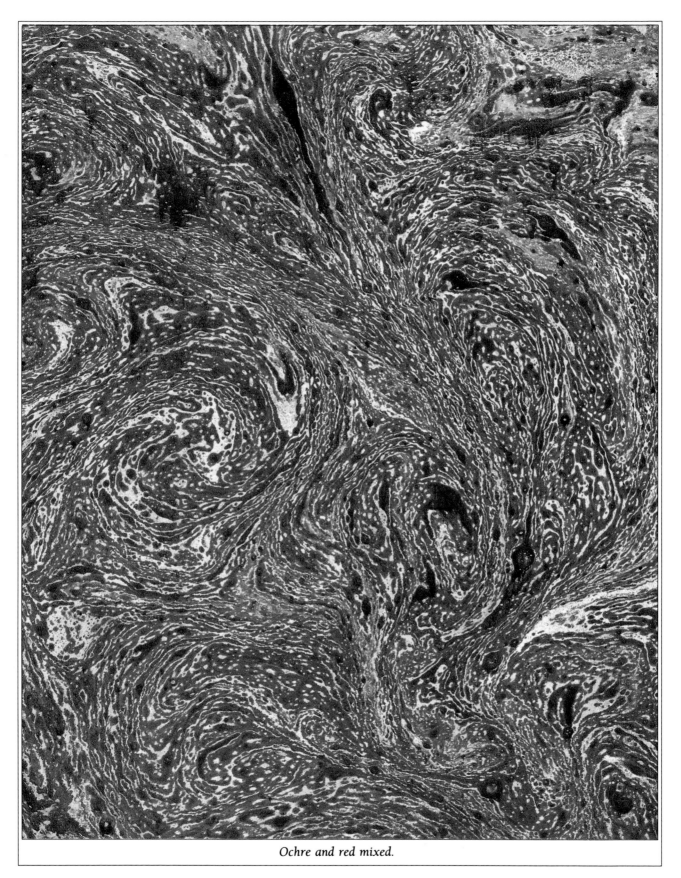

Ochre and red mixed.

Yellow ochre, indigo, red.

Patterned

The colours are dropped on evenly, at regular intervals, rather than splattered; they can be alongside or on top of each other. The colours are then very gently but deliberately drawn through with a stylus, across the bath, and then if liked from top to bottom of the bath, forming delicate lines. There is an endless variety of patterns which can be made using this technique. For example, circles of colour can be swirled with a stylus into clover or leaf shapes, or drawn one into the other to form a continuous patterned line.

An example of a patterned effect as it appears on the surface of the bath.

Yellow, indigo.

Yellow ochre, indigo, red.

Yellow ochre, indigo, red.

Yellow, blue.

Bands of red, indigo, and yellow ochre.

Combed

It is advisable to have a slightly thicker size in the bath for this, so that the combing can hold its shape. Bands of colour are dropped on to the surface of the bath in a regular sequence. The comb is then lightly but evenly drawn through the top surface of the bath: do not immerse the comb too deeply, or it will pull the colours. This combed surface can be further manipulated by pulling a stylus through the surface at regular intervals, creating a variation on the traditional French curl or snail pattern.

An example of a combed effect as it appears on the surface of the bath.

Bands of green, yellow, red, and indigo.

Bands of green, yellow, red, and indigo, combed through and then manipulated with a stylus.

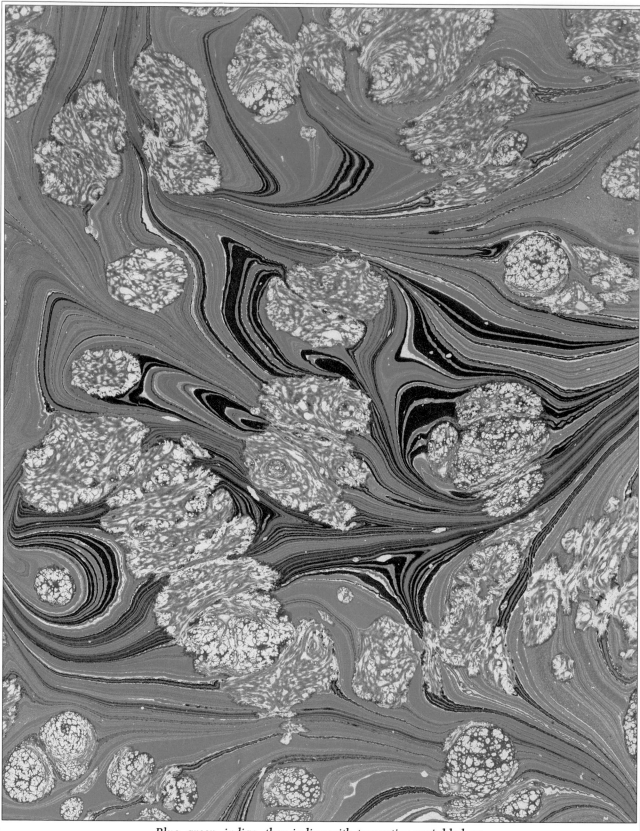

Blue, green, indigo, then indigo with turpentine sprinkled on.

Stormont

The colours are dropped on as for stone marble or splatter, and then lightly drawn through with a stylus to form lines or vein colours. The last colour, usually indigo, has a drop of detergent or spirits of soap (from a chemist) or pure turpentine added to it. When this is thrown on to the surface on top of the vein colours, it falls in lacy-like drops, which is typical of this classic pattern.

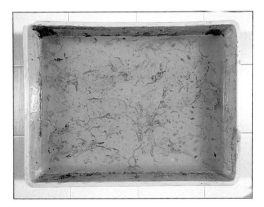

An example of a Stormont pattern as it appears on the surface of the bath.

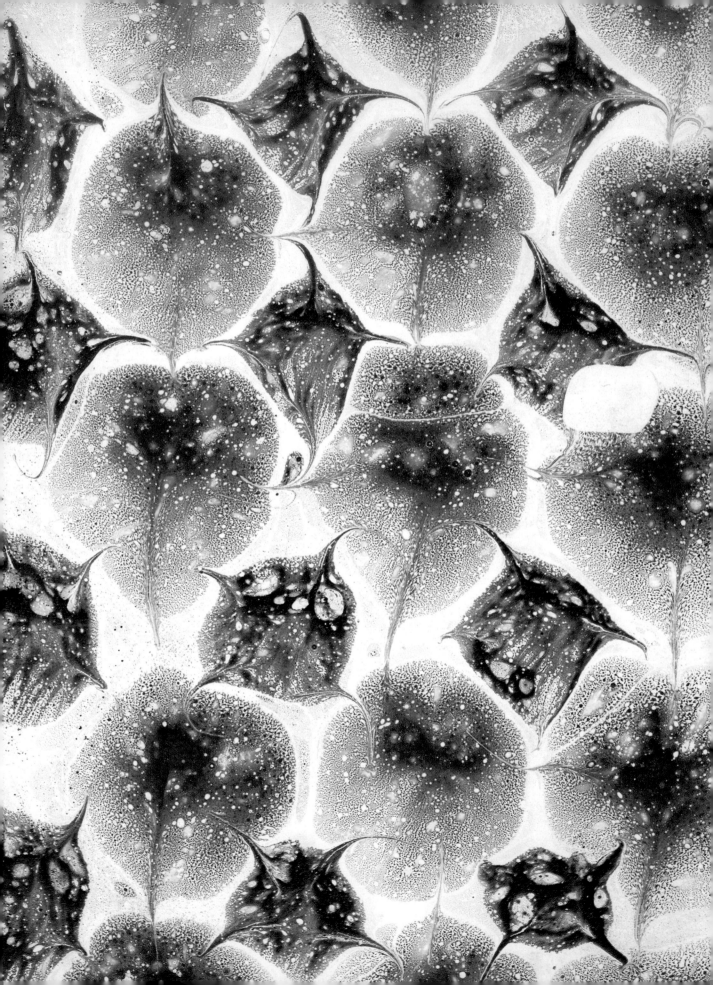

EXPERIMENTAL
MARBLING
TECHNIQUES

Rose dropped on, then green dropped between and tweaked into stalks.

Experimental
marbling techniques

It is better to approach the experimental side of marbling once you are fairly experienced in the traditional method. You will probably find that, whilst doing the latter, you have occasionally created some rather odd papers quite unintentionally. For example, if you have forgotten to clean the bath between marbling, then you will find that the colours remaining on the surface inhibit the new colours you throw down, causing them to form odd shapes, instead of the more usual circles. You can do this deliberately, by letting old colours build up on the surface.

Another interesting experiment is to sprinkle a little detergent, neat or diluted, on the surface, which causes the colours to disperse. If this is left for some time, and not immediately taken up, then the colours move and shift in a strange way.

You can also vary the consistency of the bath itself, making it thicker to inhibit the spread of the colours, or making it so thick that the colours can actually be brushed on to the surface. The French marbler, Marie-Ange Doizey, uses this technique, brushing on bands of colour with thin 5cm (2in) wide brushes, which she can then comb or manipulate with a stylus.

The most innovative oil marbler I know is David Wade, and the illustration on page 57 shows a most extraordinary paper he made, by putting the bath on a slowly turning surface (I think in this instance a typist's revolving chair), and rotating it so that the colours formed a circle. I must confess that I have never managed to do this myself.

As you will see, once you have mastered the basic technique of marbling with oil paints, the possibilities are almost limitless, and there is always great pleasure in making new discoveries and producing unusual papers.

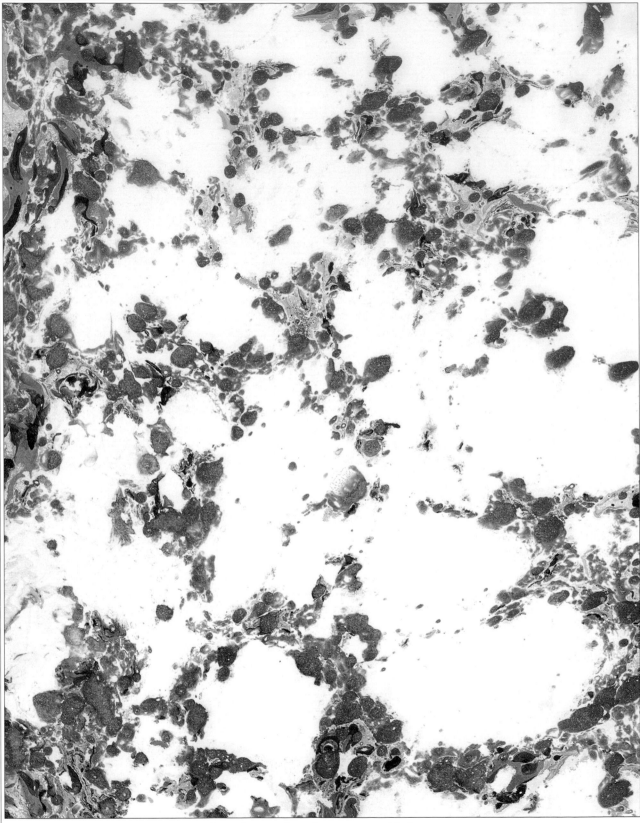

Grey, brown, then detergent sprinkled on.

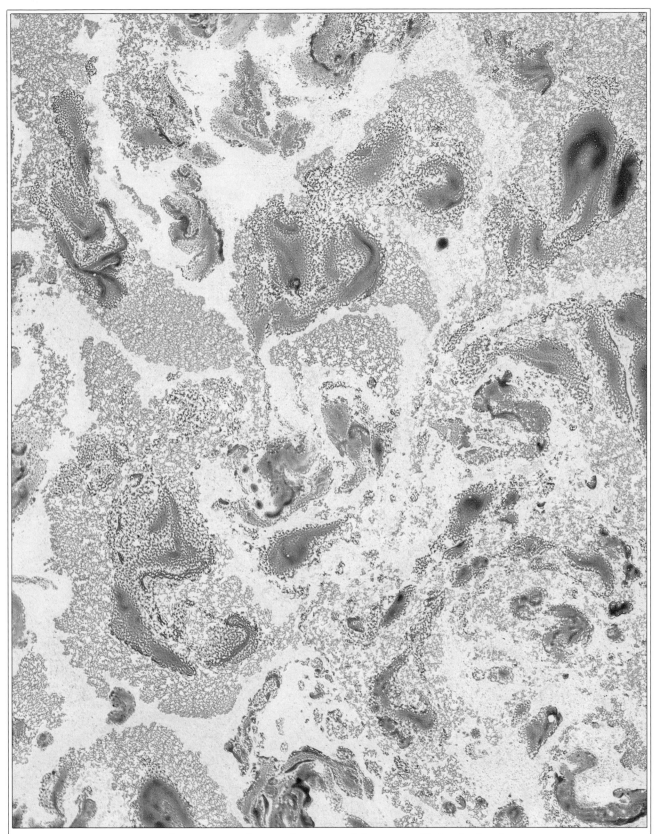

Rose, then green, with a small amount of detergent added to both colours.

Yellow, red, light blue, dark blue, then detergent thrown on.

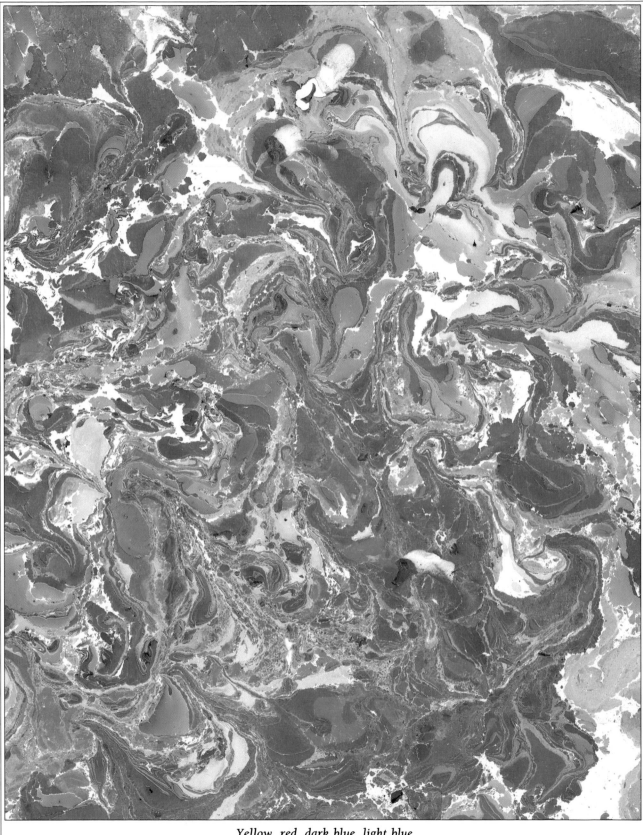

Yellow, red, dark blue, light blue.

[55]

Black all over, then blue thrown on and piled up to give a splintered effect.

Red, then blue, using a centrifugal force. Paper by David Wade.

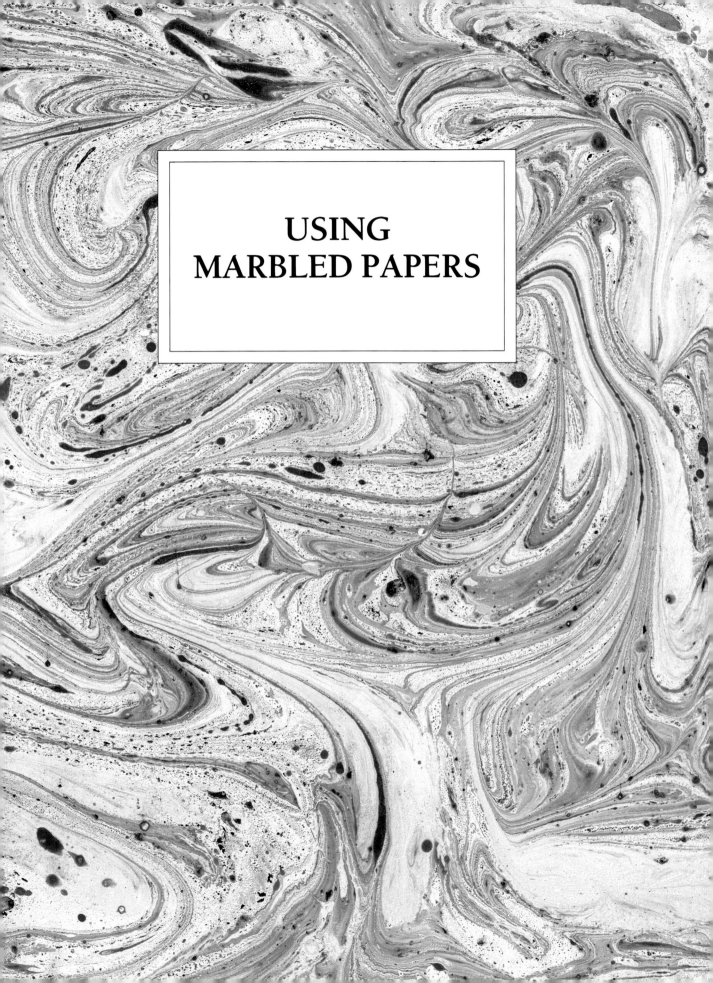

USING
MARBLED PAPERS

Lampshade and book covered with marbled paper.

Using marbled papers

In the seventeenth and eighteenth centuries, decorated papers were widely used to bind books, to line cupboards and boxes, and to embellish walls. Nowadays, wide use is made of printed decorated paper for gift wrapping, and for covering articles of stationery, but it is particularly satisfying to be able to make, and use, your own individual paper – especially as no two papers can ever be exactly alike!

Quite small pieces, salvaged from a not entirely satisfactory sheet, can be used to make birthday or Christmas cards, or tiny little carrier-bags to be filled with chocolates. With larger sized sheets, the possibilities are almost endless. Covers can be made for books; cardboard containers or coffee tins can be covered; blotters, pencil holders with matching covered pencils, lampshades, concertina files, cookery recipe boxes, and sweet containers are some of the other ideas that spring to mind. One of the most ingenious uses that I have seen was by an ex-student, who sent me a Christmas jigsaw puzzle of marbled paper, with the message written in coloured ink (see page 63).

Pencils, containers and book covered with marbled paper.

Portfolio and jigsaw puzzle made from marbled paper.

Index

Alum 7
Antique spot 23

Beeswax 7
Brushes 10–12, 14, 51

Card 10, 17, 23
Carragheen 7, 12
Colour mixing 12–14
Combed
    papers 42–5
    pattern on bath 43
Combs 10–11, 17, 43, 51
    wide-toothed 11

Detergent 11–12. 47, 51–4

Ebru 7
Equipment 10–11
Experimental marbling techniques 49–57
Eye-droppers 10–11, 14

French
    curl 23, 43
    shell 23
    snail 23, 43

Gum tragacanth 7

How to begin 9–19

Italian shell 23

Knitting needles 10–11

Marble cut
    papers 30–5
    pattern on bath 31
Marbling with oil paints 14–19
Materials 11–13
Monotone marbled effect 31

Newspaper 10–11, 14–15, 17, 19

Oil colours 7, 11–19, 23, 31, 37, 43, 47, 51
Ox-gall 7

Paint pots 10–11, 14
Paper 11–12, 15, 18–19
Patterned
    papers 36–41
    pattern on bath 37
Pine resin 7

Rags 10–11, 15

Size, see water-thickener
Spirits of soap 47
Splatter
    papers, see stone marble
    pattern on bath, see stone marble
Stone marble 47
    papers 22–9
    pattern on bath 23
Stormont 23
    papers 46–7
    pattern on bath 47
Straws 11
Stylus 7, 10–11, 15, 17, 23, 31, 37, 43, 47, 51
Suminagashi 7
Surface tension 15

Traditional marbling techniques 21–47
    combed 42–5
    marble cut 30–5
    patterned 36–41
    stone marble 22–9
    Stormont 46–7
Tray, watertight 10–11, 14
Turpentine 7, 11–15, 23, 31, 47

Using marbled papers 59–63
    books 60, 62
    containers 62
    jigsaw puzzle 63
    lampshade 60
    pencils 62
    portfolio 63

Vein colours 23, 47

Washing-up liquid, see detergent
Water-thickener 7, 11–12, 14, 18, 43, 51
    cornflour 11
    gelatine 11
    gomme de guar 12
    powdered carragheen 12
    PVA 12
    wallpaper paste 11
Work surface 10, 14